SAINT JOHN SOUTHWORTH

NICHOLAS SCHOFIELD & GERARD SKINNER

Saint John Southworth

The Parish Priest of Westminster

Cover picture: Icon of St John Southworth © Westminster Cathedral
Photo by Martin Smith
Cover design: DX Imaging
Illustrations courtesy of The Westminster Diocesan Archives

ST PAULS Publishing
187 Battersea Bridge Road, London SW11 3AS, UK
www.stpaulspublishing.com

ISBN 978-0-85439-824-9

A catalogue record is available for this book from the British Library.

Set by Tukan DTP, Stubbington, Fareham, UK
Printed in Slovenia

ST PAULS is an activity of the priests and brothers
of the Society of St Paul who proclaim the Gospel
through the media of social communication.

Contents

Introduction

VISITORS TO Westminster Cathedral can hardly fail to notice the body of St John Southworth in the Chapel of St George and the English Martyrs.

He is dressed in priestly vestments and a silver mask covers his face. He was one of the many English Catholic priests of the sixteenth and seventeenth centuries who laboured secretly before being imprisoned, tried and executed, simply for being priests. In this sense he is a representative of several generations of English priests.

However, as the famous convert and writer, Mgr Ronald Knox, noted in a 1954 sermon at the Cathedral, St John Southworth also stands apart: 'the only one of our English martyrs to suffer under a dictatorship [of Oliver Cromwell]. The only one who notoriously pleaded guilty to being a priest. The only one, so far, whose body is preserved to us entire.' He was also the last secular priest to be put to death in England.

As with so many of the English martyrs, so much of St John Southworth's life and work is known only to God and to those for whom he laboured. However, the story of his relics must be amongst the most intriguing and well documented accounts of any martyr of the time.

In writing this book we must acknowledge the work of the saint's previous biographers, especially Fr Albert B. Purdie, who so fully and carefully recorded the recovery of his relics for Westminster Cathedral. We also wish to acknowledge the generous assistance of Gaynor Brown, Stephen Moseling and Miriam Power, the Archivist at Westminster Cathedral.

Nicholas Schofield and Gerard Skinner

‘Good people, I was born in Lancashire’

VERY LITTLE is known about St John Southworth’s early life. Even his date of birth is uncertain. Bishop Challoner gives it as 1592, but other sources suggest that he was born in the 1580s. We know that since the fourteenth century the Southworth family had owned Samlesbury Hall, on the road between Preston and Blackburn in Lancashire, and it is often assumed that the future martyr belonged to a junior branch of the family. He was proud of his descent and opened the speech at his execution with the words, ‘Good people, I was born in Lancashire.’

Nor do we know what sort of education he received as a youth, though it is likely to have been centred on one of the Catholic safe houses which were so numerous in Elizabethan Lancashire. In 1592 an apostate priest named Dingley reported to the government that a Catholic schoolmaster was living at Samlesbury Hall, perhaps this unnamed individual taught the young John. Alternatively he may have attended a local institution, such as the grammar school at Senely Green, which produced another martyr, St Edmund Arrowsmith.

As a youth John Southworth would have attended the secret Masses celebrated by visiting priests, using various aliases and disguises, and only dressing as a priest at the altar. He knew from his own family the price that Catholics paid for loyalty to the ancient faith. A good example is provided by the owner of Samlesbury Hall himself, Sir John Southworth, of whom it was said that no layman had suffered more in fines and imprisonment for the Faith. He was first imprisoned in 1568 and spent the rest of his life in and out of confinement, and under the watchful eyes of the authorities. A search of the house in 1592 revealed a number of 'superstitious things':

> ...one canopy to hang over the altar, found in a vault over the drawing-room; two brass candlesticks, after a superstitious fashion; fourteen images of various fashions;... thirteen books of papistry, that is to say, a *Rheims Testament*; *An Apology for the English Seminaries*; *A defence for the Censure upon the Rev. Edmund Campion's two books*; *A Treatise on Schism*; *A Discourse of John Nicholls*; all the rest of the books are in manuscript.

Several of Sir John's sons studied in the Catholic colleges overseas, including Christopher, who entered the English College, Rome, and was arrested soon after returning to England as a priest in December 1586. He spent the next fourteen years behind bars, mostly at Wisbech Castle, but probably ended his days as chaplain at Samlesbury Hall.

Joannes Southworthus Lancastrensis

ST JOHN SOUTHWORTH first enters recorded history on 14 July 1613. According to the register of the English College, Douai:

> *1613 Die 14 Julii...eodem etiam die receptus est in Collegium ut convictor Joannes Southworthus Lancastrensis, hic dictus Lee.*

> 1613 14 July…John Southworth of Lancashire, here known as Lee, was received into the college as a convictor.

Students invariably used an alias to protect their identity and it is possible that 'Lee' was the family name of John's mother. Students at Douai could be either *alumni* or *convictores*; the first category were those sponsored by the papal pension, while *con-victores,* such as Southworth, were supported by their families or bursaries funded by clergy or friends.

William Allen, the future cardinal, had opened the English College on 29 September 1568. Douai seemed a good location for such an enterprise. Situated near the English Channel, the university had recently received its charter from Philip II of Spain and was already the home to many English exiles. Initially it aimed to unite the English Catholic

Diaspora and provide the resources for Catholic scholarship that could no longer be found at Oxford and Cambridge. The Jesuit Fr Persons affirmed that 'there was no intention at all (as I have often heard Dr Allen affirm) of the end of returning again into their country to teach and preach.' However, it is perhaps natural that the eyes of the exiles should have begun to look longingly to the other side of the channel, especially as numbers increased and those who had completed their studies had little to do.

The college thus became a celebrated seminary, the first in the Anglophone world, and produced a new type of missionary: the 'seminary priest', highly trained in theology and controversy, and eager to return to his homeland, despite the obvious dangers. In 1577 St Cuthbert Mayne became the first 'seminary priest' to be hanged, drawn and quartered. Nearly two-thirds were imprisoned at some point and a total of 116 were executed during Elizabeth's reign alone.

The first years of the college were marked by financial difficulties and concerns surrounding security – it proved easy enough for the English authorities to plant spies, and this led to the custom of students and staff adopting aliases. Further trouble was caused by the fact the Low Countries were a hothouse of religious divisions. Indeed, for most of its history the college was affected by the seesaw of European politics, and between 1578 and 1593 the college was relocated to Rheims.

What was life like at the English College? As might be expected, there was daily Mass, weekly reception of Holy Communion, prayer using the method of St Ignatius Loyola and twice weekly fasting for 'the conversion of England'. The academic syllabus was partly influenced by the Jesuits and included a comprehensive grounding in scholastic theology (particularly that of St Thomas Aquinas) but it was adapted to suit future missionaries in Protestant England. Much attention was paid to preaching, disputation and the study of Sacred Scripture, the chief 'weapon' used by Protestant controversialists. The timetable included daily Scriptural lectures, classes in the Biblical languages, readings from the holy book at meal times and regular debates on disputed points.

On 24 May 1614 Southworth received the tonsure, the first step on the road to ordination, and in December of that year was admitted formally as an *alumnus* of the College, promising that 'I am ready and will be ever ready, so far as His most holy grace shall help me, to receive Holy Orders in due time and to return to England in order to gain the souls of others as often and when it shall seem good to the Superior of the College so to command.'

However, in May 1616 Southworth was obliged to convalesce in England, presumably at his Lancashire home. Conditions at the college were harsh and illness was a common occurrence. Many students returned home for reasons of health and some unfortunates died at Douai from dysentery and fever. Shortly after Southworth's arrival back at Douai in the spring of 1617, the dreaded plague hit the town. Students were confined to the college as a precaution and some 'escaped' to nearby Cambrai. In later life Southworth would gain further first-hand experience of the sufferings of plague victims in London.

Despite such scares, Southworth proceeded in his studies. He received minor orders at Cambrai in September 1617 and was finally ordained priest on Holy Saturday 1618, having received the sub-diaconate and diaconate over the previous few weeks. The future martyr celebrated his first Mass in the College chapel on Easter Sunday, 'with great affection of devotion'.

DOUAI COLLEGE
IN THE TIME OF ST JOHN SOUTHWORTH

In Vineam Anglicanam

SOUTHWORTH REMAINED at Douai for a further year to complete his academic studies. During this time doubts began to emerge in his mind about his future in the secular priesthood and, on 28 June 1619, he left Douai for a Benedictine house, where he could test his monastic calling. The documents are silent as to where this monastery was located but he did not stay long. The College *Diary* records that on 13 December he left Douai *in vineam Anglicanam*, 'to the Vineyard of England.'

Southworth is representative of the many mission priests of the time because we know very little about his labours. His was a priestly life lived discreetly, travelling between the various 'safe houses', celebrating Mass and administering the sacraments, teaching the Faith and praying for England's conversion. The lack of available information may also indicate that his early priestly ministry was relatively uneventful, without the adventures so often associated with pursuivants and hiding-holes. Indeed, these years were relatively stable for Catholics and Southworth may have been left largely to his own devices. Persecution tended to peak during moments of national crisis. There could be periods of uneasy toleration, when it was more expedient for the authorities to turn a blind eye to recusancy. The last priest to be executed during the reign of James I, Blessed William Southerne, suffered at Newcastle-under-Lyme in April 1618. Shortly afterwards complex diplomatic negotiations were begun to arrange the marriage of the heir to the throne, the future Charles I, to the Spanish Infanta. This fitted in with King James' dream of acting as an international peacemaker and resolving the Thirty Years War, which was tearing Europe apart and had proved disastrous for his son-in-law, the Elector Palatine.

The negotiations lasted five years. Spain and the Papacy insisted that full toleration of English Catholics was necessary if the marriage was to be arranged and, although no positive legislation was passed, the penal laws were relaxed. Moreover, the English Catholics were even granted their first bishop since the reign of Mary I: the appropriately named William Bishop, who became Vicar Apostolic of England in 1623. In the same year the English Jesuits were given their own Province, divided into twelve districts, which further promised a future of tolerance and co-existence.

The extent to which Catholics were able to practice their Faith in London is revealed by the so-called 'Doleful Evensong' of 26 October 1623. As many as three hundred Catholics packed into a large room at the French Embassy, situated in the old Blackfriars, to hear a renowned Jesuit preacher, Fr Drury. The weight of the congregation was too much for the floor, which collapsed during the service, claiming the lives of the preacher and around ninety others. Some of the victims were buried at St Etheldreda's, Ely Place, which was then being used by the Spanish Ambassador.

Southworth seems to have been mainly based in London and the sole reference to these years of his priesthood comes from an anti-Catholic pamphlet, *The Foot Out of the Snare* (1624), written by the apostate John Gee. This includes a list of 'Romish priests and Jesuits now resident about the city of London', among whom is 'Southworth and Southworth, both secular priests.' This is a confusing statement, for John Southworth was the only known secular priest with that surname at the time. It is possible that the other 'Southworth' was the Jesuit Nathaniel Bacon, who often used the alias 'Southwell'.

By the time Gee's work was published in April 1624, however, Southworth was back on the continent and in July he was acting as temporary chaplain to the English Benedictine nuns of Brussels. The convent of the Glorious Assumption of Our Lady was the first house for English religious women to be founded overseas after the Reformation, established in 1598 by Lady Mary Percy, the daughter of Blessed Thomas Percy, the Earl of Northumberland, who was executed after the Northern Rebellion of 1569. The nuns at Brussels included representatives from many well-known Catholic families, such as the Arundells, Gages and Knatchbulls, and the community even included Dame Mary Persons, the niece of Fr Robert Persons, the well-known Jesuit controversialist.

'God's own country'

IN 1626 SOUTHWORTH returned to England and took up residence in his native Lancashire. During the priest's absence overseas, Charles I had succeeded to the throne. His consort, Henrietta Maria, was a French Catholic and to many the future seemed hopeful. However, the presence of the Queen's Catholic chaplains at court and the lull in persecution occasioned by the 'Spanish Match' led to fresh clamours for the observance of the penal laws.

Southworth was arrested soon after his arrival in England and taken to Lancaster Castle, where he was tried and condemned to death. It seems that he was granted a reprieve and was still at Lancaster in 1628 when another condemned priest, St Edmund Arrowsmith, was brought in chains. He had been betrayed by a young man whom he had reproved for 'an incestuous marriage' and captured at Brindle Moss, a few miles distant from Samlesbury. Southworth was able to console him as he awaited execution.

> As he was being led through the castle yard, a worthy and venerable priest, his fellow-prisoner, who had been condemned for his faith a year before, but stood then reprieved, showed himself to Father Arrowsmith from a large window. The Martyr, as

> soon as he perceived him, asked for the last absolution by lifting up his hands (the sign they had mutually agreed upon), in order that, being sent forth by the servant of Jesus Christ, with comfort from on high, he might endure in the day of battle and triumph in the conflict. This priest was the Rev. Mr Southworth, who absolved him before all the multitude, and bid him with the sign of Redemption, pass on to conquest and a crown of glory.

Arrowsmith was hanged, drawn and quartered on 28 August 1628 and it seems that Southworth's father was present by the gallows, for he later told his son about the priest's last moments. According to a contemporary document, Southworth 'did sincerely protest that in the window of his chamber he saw a most resplendent brightness, such an one as in all his life he never saw before, which did show itself from the prison unto the gallows, as if it had been a glistening glow, and the sun at that time was obscured with clouds, and the most part of that day likewise.' A third priest was being held at Lancaster, the Benedictine St Ambrose Barlow, also from Lancashire, who joined Southworth in assisting Arrowsmith to prepare for death.

Soon afterwards Southworth was ordered to be taken to Wisbech Castle in Cambridgeshire, where many priests had been confined, though it is unlikely that he was ever moved there. By April 1630 he was in London in the Clink, a prison dating back to the twelfth century and situated on the south bank of the

Thames, near the present Blackfriars Bridge. His name was included among a list of sixteen priests who were to be banished overseas. Once again, this seems not to have happened – or, as Challoner notes, 'if ever he went abroad, he quickly returned to his Master's work.'

The Clink was at least an easy-going prison and Southworth was able to leave the prison on parole and minister to the Catholics of London. The anti-Catholic Prynne noted that Southworth 'had free liberty to walke abroad at his pleasure (as most priests during their imprisonment, had, the more safely to seduce His Majesties good subjects, and open Masses in their prisons to boote)'. Three decades previously, when the Jesuit, John Gerard, was transferred to the Clink, he compared the move to 'a translation from Purgatory to Paradise': 'I no longer heard obscene and bawdy songs, but, instead, I had Catholics praying in the next cell.' Gerard had been able to say Mass daily and reconciled many to the Faith, including the future martyr St John Rigby. Indeed, 'so many Catholics came to visit me that there were often as many as six or eight people at a time waiting their turn to see me.'

Southworth was able to keep up with ecclesiastical politics while in the Clink. The second Vicar Apostolic of England, Bishop Richard Smith, had been a divisive figure and was first suspended from office and then, in 1629, forced to flee to France, where he spent part of his exile under the protection of Cardinal Richelieu. The resulting power vacuum was filled by the Chapter of Secular Clergy, which had been established by the first Vicar Apostolic, William Bishop, though with uncertain canonical standing. Southworth was one of twenty-four signatories of a letter to Bishop Smith dated 19 July 1632 begging him to return to England, where there was a great need of episcopal government. Shortly afterwards Southworth signed a petition addressed to the Pope asking for Smith's return, with a strengthened authority, so that order could be imposed on the chaos. However, Smith never did return and there would be no bishop resident in England for the remainder of Southworth's life.

As well as spending time in the Clink, Southworth seems to have been moved at some stage to the Gatehouse prison at Westminster, where he had 'a silver key to get out and exercise his priestly ministry.' This suggests that he was able to bribe the keeper and that he also had some financial means on which he could draw. Indeed, he was able to afford a servant, John Lillie, and donate £200 on one occasion to the Chapter of the Secular Clergy.

‘The greatness of this calamity exceedeth all belief’

PLAGUE WAS a regular occurrence in an over-crowded city like London. 1665, of course, was the year of the ‘Great Plague’, killing perhaps 20 percent of the city’s population, but this was remembered not only because of its severity but also because it was the last major plague epidemic to strike London. Given the notoriety of the 1665 outbreak, it is easy to forget that the disease found victims on an annual basis during the early modern period and that serious epidemics happened roughly once a decade in the early seventeenth century. During the relatively minor outbreak of 1517, St Thomas More even commented that London had become more dangerous than a battlefield.

Moreover, plague was a European problem. The early seventeenth century saw massive outbreaks across the continent, caused in part by the frequent movement of armies and their entourages during the bloody Thirty Years War. Although England had only a limited involvement in such hostilities, as many as 20,000 Britons served overseas during the reigns of James I and Charles I, and London remained a major port and commercial centre.

Contemporary medicine was ill-equipped to deal

with the disease and the response of the authorities was to lock up plague-stricken houses, together with the inhabitants, both sick and healthy, until the epidemic passed. The doors were famously marked with a blue or red headless St Anthony's cross and the words 'Lord have mercy upon us'. Those who had come into any contact with the sick carried a long white pole. Meanwhile, provisions and assistance were often provided by the local parish, which remained a unit of both religious and civil administration.

In Catholic countries such practical actions were combined with penitential processions, special services and the invocation of the saints; St Sebastian and St Roch were particularly popular, as were the local patron saints. Travelling around Europe, it is still possible to find churches and monuments erected in thanksgiving by survivors of the plague, such as the magnificent Venetian churches of the Redentore and Santa Maria della Salute or the Pestsäule (plague column) in Vienna, showing the Holy Trinity surrounded by the choirs of angels. Likewise, the famous Passion Play at Oberammergau originated with a vow made by the villagers during a plague outbreak in 1633.

In Protestant England the expression of people's faith was more sober, though nonetheless heartfelt. There were prayers for deliverance from the plague and periods of fasting in the event of an epidemic. Instructions were given, however, for the shortening of church services, 'because such detaining of the people so long together may prove dangerous to the further increase of the Sicknesse.' The plague was inevitably interpreted as divine punishment for sin, immorality and corruption – and in London 'popery' was sometimes blamed. When the plague hit the city in 1630, for example, puritans like William Gouge pointed an accusing finger at the presence of Catholicism at Court and the Catholicising sympathies of Archbishop Laud within the Church of England.

St John Southworth was intimately involved with tending the sick during the plague of 1636, which cost the lives of over 12,000 Londoners. The usual plague legislation had been put into effect that April and orders given for the building of pest-houses to house the sick. The King even consented for the release of those in the debtors' prisons. Infected houses were quarantined, as was usual – 324 houses containing 1,328 individuals in the parish of St Martin's-in-the-Fields alone. The disease was no respecter of class or creed. Catholics suffered alongside Protestants but were particularly vulnerable since they could not benefit so easily from the help arranged by the (Anglican) parishes. A Catholic living in Bloomsbury, Cecily Crowe, complained that assistance was not given despite the fact that many recusants contributed to the parish rate. It seems that many Catholics defied the enforced quarantine since they thought it was 'a matter of conscience to visit their neighbours in any sickness, yea, though they know it to be infection; even the red cross does not keep them out.'

The crisis was such as to bring together two elements of the Catholic community that were normally in disagreement with each other – the Jesuits and the secular clergy – and they each chose a priest to minister to the plague victims and collect alms: St John Southworth and St Henry Morse (a Jesuit). The two men had actually overlapped for a while at Douai and now they became reacquainted. Some preparation was needed, both spiritual (we know that Morse spent a short time in retreat, following St Ignatius' *Spiritual Exercises*, before beginning his labours) and practical. A list was compiled of the Catholics known to be living in London and it was decided that Southworth would concentrate on the area between Westminster Abbey and St James', while Morse would work around St Giles-in-the-Fields. Both places were densely-populated, poverty-stricken and contained a rabbit-warren of alleys and lanes. Indeed, things had not changed over two centuries later when plans were being drawn up for the construction of Westminster Cathedral. Mgr Charles Edward Brown, a long-serving Cathedral Sub-Administrator, later recalled that 'Westminster was a very different place in those days from what it is now; it was full of slums, courts and back alleys and streets that no respectable person would venture down after dark. Policemen walked in pairs for safety's sake and many of the "natives" lived more like animals than human beings in lofts above old stables...There was at that time a serious outbreak of smallpox in the district; we actually had one case in Archbishop's House (the odd-job man). The consequence was that we all had to be vaccinated, from the Cardinal [Vaughan] downwards.'

These were the conditions with which Southworth and Morse would have been familiar.

It is perhaps little surprising that there were initial tensions between Morse and Southworth, since for well over half a century there had been dissension between the Jesuits and the secular clergy – largely conflicts over differing visions for the English Church and ecclesiastical jurisdictions, as well as rivalry in the mission field. We read in a contemporary Jesuit document that:

> Father Morse, in the first days of his attendance on the sick, whether overpowered at the outset by the formidable and noisome symptoms of the disease, or anxious to leave none of the daily increasing number of patients without the necessary help, or else deeming it prudent to avoid a less necessary danger, satisfied himself with administering the Sacraments of Penance and of the Blessed Eucharist, and omitted that of Extreme Unction. His secular coadjutor [Southworth] hearing of this omission, began to complain of what he called the unworthy timidity of his fellow-labourer. But Father Morse, hearing of this report, submitted to the charge with religious humility, and, blaming none but himself, at once discarded his apprehensions and administered to the infected all the aids of religion.

Like many seculars, Southworth also raised doubts about the validity of the Jesuits' faculties and discouraged people from going to confession to Morse. The Jesuit, unsurprisingly, confronted him about this and they came to some sort of agreement, which allowed them to work together. Indeed, when Morse contracted the plague himself, Southworth briefly shouldered the burden of the whole enterprise until the Jesuit recovered.

The two priests had decided that 'their first endeavour should be to induce the sick to reconcile themselves to God by the sacrament of Penance, and that for the relief of their corporeal necessities, whatever alms might be procured by either party should be placed in a common stock, from which the most necessitous should be indiscriminately relieved.' They wore a 'distinctive mark' on their clothing and carried the traditional white rod. As well as administering the sacraments and providing spiritual comfort, they helped distribute alms, provisions and medication and visited all those who asked for them, including many non-Catholics.

The Annual Letters of the English Province of the Society of Jesus give us many details of Morse's ministry and a glimpse of what Southworth must himself have experienced. The conditions in which they worked were harsh. On one occasion Morse found a young man lying on a bed in 'a most loathsome place, against which every natural feeling revolted as he sat down to hear his confession, compelled to hold his ear close to him for fear of being overheard. But the Divine Goodness at once compensated the Father for this self-denial, for so great a light was vouchsafed to the sick man to discover the heinousness of his sins, that his utterance was nearly choked with tears and sobs.' It is reported that fifty Protestant families were reconciled by

Morse to the Church. Many went to confession – including some who 'had been to confession to the Capuchin Fathers serving the Queen's Chapel; but in the doubt whether they had been rightly understood (for these foreign Fathers were incapable of doing so perfectly) they preferred to confess a second time to Father Morse. The secular priest,' the report goes on, 'also frequently and with pain complained to our Fathers of the same thing.'

The work of the two priests did not go unnoticed. The Anglican curate of St Margaret's, Westminster, complained about the work of Southworth (whom he misnamed 'Southwell') in his parish:

> This Southwell, under a pretence of distributing alms sent from some of the priests in Somerset House and other papists, doth take occasion to go into divers visited houses in Westminster, and namely to the houses of one William Baldwin and William Stiles in the Kemp-Yard in Westminster, and there finding Baldwin near the point of death did set upon him by all means to make him change his religion, whereunto by subtle persuasions Baldwin easily consented and received the sacrament from him according to the Church of Rome, and so died Romish Catholic. And in the same manner he perverted William Stiles who also died a Romish Catholic. And Southwell, to colour and hide these wicked practices, doth fee the watchman and other poor people thereabouts that they should affirm he comes only to give alms. And thus under pretence of relieving the bodies of poor people he poisons their souls.

The curate asked for 'some speedy course' to be taken against the priest and to prevent 'divers poor people, newly turned Romish Catholic' from hearing Mass in the Queen's chapel at Denmark House. 'And three of those poor people', he continued, 'watched all night with William Stiles immediately before he died and the next day went thither to Mass; a most wicked course if it should not be remedied.' The curate's complaint interestingly states that Southworth 'long hath been a prisoner in the Gatehouse, but lives about Clerkenwell'.

As a result of these allegations Southworth was more closely confined in the Gatehouse. This did not prevent him from publishing a joint appeal with Morse in October 1636 'To the Catholickes of England':

> Right Honourable, Right Worshipful, and
> Much Respected:
>
> We underwritten being appointed to serve the infected Catholics of the City and Suburbs of London, with our spiritual assistance, having seen with our eyes the extreme necessity which many of the poorer sort are fallen into, by reason of the present sickness, do think ourselves obliged even in conscience, to make the same known to you, by a public letter, to the end that those, whom God hath blest with sufficient ability and means, taking so weighty a matter into their serious consideration, may, through the help of his holy grace, resolve with themselves forthwith, to do what in them lieth, and what in such an exigent Christian charity and

duty bindeth every one unto, for the necessary support and relief of so great a multitude.

We do protest unto you seriously, even upon our souls and consciences, that the greatness of this calamity exceedeth all belief, in so many as we should never have imagined the least part, of that which really is, had our own eyes, and daily experience sufficiently attested the same unto us, and we truly aver, that this so great a desolation amongst our poor brethren, joined with the small means and power we have to relieve them, is a far more grievous affliction unto us, than all the labours and dangers, which we undergo daily for their spiritual aid and comfort.

There are some persons in the number of these afflicted, who, notwithstanding they were well born and bred, having been constrained, through extremity of want, to sell or pawn all they had, remain shut up within the bare walls of a poor chamber, having not wherewithal to allay the rage of hunger, nor scarcely to cover nakedness. There are others, who, for the space of three days together have not gotten a morsel of bread to put into their mouths. We have just cause to fear that some do perish for want of food: others for want of tendance: others for want of ordinary helps and remedies, with which they might easily escape death, and be cured. At this present there are about fifty several families, which are visited, and shut up; and truly such is the feeling which many of these poor creatures have, of this their most wretched state, that finding themselves deprived of means whereby to live, (all manner of work failing them at this time) they are brought even to the brink of despair, wishing from their heart to be seized upon with the sickness (if God were so pleased) thereby to hasten death, and with it, the end of this their languishing pain, which to them is worse than death itself.

The example of the Protestants, both in the City and the Country (which is well known to all) may be no small inducement upon Catholics to imitate their care, providence, and bounty in this behalf. We have heard of some particulars amongst them, which are very memorable. One noble man of theirs hath bestowed lately the sum of three hundred pounds, leaving it to the distribution of a Gentleman of good quality, who took the pains to visit the houses of the poor himself, and to divide it amongst them with his own hands. An other party of account (Son to an Alderman of London) hath been seen to go in person to seek out the poor that wanted work, being neighbours to such as were infected, and with his own hands to bestow a large benevolence amongst them. And if those who acknowledge no merit in good works, out of a generous mind or natural compassion are so ready to assist their distressed brethren so plentifully; it may seem that no less, but rather much more should be expected at the hands of Catholics, who professing to believe the doctrine of merit, have thereby a far higher motive than Protestants have to perform works of Charity, and to open the bowels of mercy, especially in a time of so general and pressing necessity, towards their poor and desolate brethren, who have no expectation of hope of relief from any, but from them alone.

This public Declaration we have judged necessary to make to all English Catholics, particularly to those that are of ability, for the discharge of our own souls, requesting, or rather conjuring all in general, and every one in particular by the bowels of our Saviour Jesus Christ to make it their own case, and to have that saying of S. John the Evangelist always before their eyes, *He that shall have the substance of the world, and shall see his brother have need, and shall shut his bowels from him; how doth the Charity of God abide in him?*

6. of October, 1636
Permissu Superiorum I.S. H.M.

Collections were made throughout the kingdom and remarkably the Queen herself contributed five hundred gold crowns – a testament to Catholic influences at Court and to the sensitive language of the appeal, which praised the charitable work of Protestants. The fund soon became known as 'Her Majesty's Alms'.

Morse himself reported several narrow escapes from arrest and imprisonment. On one occasion a kindly magistrate questioned him but released him on account of his good work. On another occasion he was returning to a house to receive a young lady into the Church. Being warned of the constables who had stationed themselves at the front door, he 'briefly instructed her as he stood at the wall, as far as time permitted, and giving her absolution, received her into the Church.' After Southworth's confinement it was Morse's time to take on the whole pastoral burden that they had once shared but his luck eventually ran out. The Jesuit was arrested and convicted, though saved from the scaffold by the Queen's intervention.

Southworth was also shown favour by King Charles I's queen, Henrietta Maria, having sent her a petition asking that he be given 'leave to goe to his frends for meanes: that hee himself may not nowe perish in prison'. It seems that his trial was postponed and he returned to his previous life of relative liberty, working among the Catholics of Westminster.

At the end of 1640, as the clouds of civil war loomed, many of the Catholic sympathisers at Court fled overseas for safety, including the Queen herself. From 1641 priests were once again being put to death, the first martyrdoms for nearly two decades. The victims of the 1640s included St Henry Morse, hanged, drawn and quartered at Tyburn on 22 January 1645. During this period we know little of Southworth, though he was probably continuing his discreet ministry and moving from one prison to another, especially the Gatehouse and Clink. He was able to attend the General Assembly of Clergy in the summer of 1653, at which he was appointed one of the collectors in London and Middlesex to raise £25 for the support of the Superior of the secular clergy and the English Agent in Rome. By this time he seems to have been closely connected with the residence of the Spanish Ambassador, one of the strongholds of London Catholicism. It seems also that he was feeling his age. We are told that:

> Mr Southworth not long before his apprehension, meeting by chance Dr Leyburn in London, who was then upon his return to Douai College, whereof he was at that time superior or president, desired with great earnestness to accompany him into Flanders, and spend the remainder of his life in retirement, being then very old. But the Doctor refused him, saying he would not deprive the nation of so zealous a missioner. Well, Sir, replied Mr Southworth, if you will not let me go with you, at least I'll follow you. Which accordingly happened, for his body was begged or bought by some friends who took care to convey it beyond the seas to the English College of Douai.

‘They have recently arrested an English priest in bed’

ST JOHN SOUTHWORTH was arrested for the final time on Monday 19 June 1654. According to Challoner it was ‘upon the information of one Jefferies, a pursuivant, whom he had in fee’ and the arresting officer was Colonel Worsley. Sometimes it was possible for priests to bribe, have ‘in fee’, pursuivants (those who hunted and entrapped priests). This was a mutually beneficial arrangement, although it left the priest very vulnerable to the kind of betrayal that ultimately happened to Southworth. The Venetian Ambassador reported:

> They have recently arrested an English priest in bed. Finding in his chamber all the requisites for the celebration of Mass, to which he intrepidly owned, they compelled him to get up and carried him off prisoner.

The indictment against Southworth reads as follows:

> The Jurors of the Lord Protector of the Commonwealth of England, Scotland, and Ireland, &c., upon their oath do present John Southworth late of the parish of Giles-in-the-Fields in the county of Middlesex was born within England, and after

> the feast of the Nativity of St John Baptist in the first year of the reign of the Lady Elizabeth late Queen of England &c., And before the nineteenth day of June in the year of Our Lord one thousand six hundred and fifty four in the parts beyond the seas was made and ordained a Priest by authority derived and pretended from the See of Rome. And that the aforesaid John Southworth the laws and statutes of England little weighing, nor the pain in them contained, any ways fearing the aforesaid nineteenth day of June in the said year of Our Lord one thousand six hundred fifty four from the parts beyond the seas aforesaid unto the Commonwealth of England to wit at the said parish of Giles-in-the-Fields in the county aforesaid on the said nineteenth day of June in the year aforesaid traitorously and as a false traitor to this Commonwealth of England did stay was and did remain against the forms of the statute in such case made and provided and against the public peace.

Two accounts of Southworth's trial are still extant. One is to be found in the Archives of the Diocese of Westminster:

> Mr Southworth on Saturday, being the 24 June 1654, was called to the bar before the Recorder of London. There he confessed himself a priest, and a condemned man many years since. On Monday the 26 he was again called to the bar and had the sentence of death pronounced against him. Upon which he desired some few words with the Court, who gave him leave and willed him to come near to

> them, which he did; and falling on his knees said: "O Lord God, I humbly thank thee, who hath made me worthy to suffer for Thy sake." Then standing up, he said: "I thank you for what you have done, and for your civilities to me, and I pray God to give you His holy grace, that you and all this nation may be converted to the true Roman, Catholic, and Apostolic Faith, and remain in heaven for ever with Jesus Christ in glory."
>
> The Recorder said: "Sir, we thank you, and will join with you in the latter part."

A second account, originally published in a pamphlet in 1687, was preserved by Challoner:

> The last Popish priest that was put to death in England for being a priest of the Romish Church was put to death in the time of Cromwell. I suppose we are not to doubt of the passionate heat which inflamed those who were then in authority against Papists and Popery. They looked upon the Papists as mortal enemies to their government, and as fast friends and devoted servants to the crown and royal family. Notwithstanding which, when the said priest came upon his trial at the sessions house in the Old Bailey, and upon his arraignment pleaded that he was not guilty of treason, but acknowledging himself a priest of the Roman Church, it clearly appeared that those who were his judges did their utmost to preserve his life, and to prevent the execution against him of those laws upon which he stood indicted; for they did for many hours suspend

> the recording of his confession, making it their endeavour to prevail with him to plead 'Not Guilty' to the indictment. They pressed him to this in the public court, assuring him that if he would so plead his life would be safe, and that they had no evidence which could prove him to be a priest. And when the old man would not be drawn to deny himself to be a priest, taking it to be a denying of his religion, and that the court was compelled to give judgment against him, the magistrate who gave the sentence was so drowned in tears upon that sad occasion, that it was long before he could pronounce the sentence which the law compelled.

John Southworth pleaded 'Not guilty to treason' but did not deny that he was a priest. Various ambassadors attempted to gain clemency from Cromwell. 'One Southworth,' recorded the royalist Richard Symonds, 'a priest long condemned to be hanged, the Portugal Ambassador went to the Lord Protector for a reprieve. "God forbid my hand should be consenting to the death of any for religion," [said Cromwell] and did promise a reprieve. The next morning he sent the Ambassador word he was sorry he could not perform his promise, for, since that, his Council had advised him that the laws should be executed to which he had sworn. And he was hanged and quartered, and the quarters the Spanish Ambassador bought off the hangman for forty shillings.' It seems that the authorities, despite any sympathy shown towards the ageing priest, felt that their hands were tied. Southworth had, after all, already been condemned to death in 1627, a sentence which had been commuted to perpetual banishment in 1630. On this occasion it had been stressed that should they [priests] be found to be present in England and Wales, then 'the Law should pass on every several person without further favour'. Indeed, as John Morrill has pointed out, 'the speed of his arraignment and execution, the fact that he was brought before the common serjeant not the high court of justice (which had been granted sole jurisdictions over treasons), and the fact that he was hanged, drawn and quartered (a recent ordinance had restricted the manner of execution to hanging only, or to beheading) all point to the fact that he died under his 1627 conviction and under the terms of his 1630 commuted sentence.' Moreover, Cromwell was unable to grant a pardon since, according to the *Instrument of Government*, he did not have this power.

The Venetian Secretary was evidently not convinced of Cromwell's sincerity, writing, 'When Cromwell was informed of this incident he seemed moved and averse from such cruelty, expressing himself, possibly from deceit or shrewdness, as opposed to violence in matters of religion and in favour of liberty of conscience for all, yet he was obliged to approve the deed and sanction this sacrifice to the law of the land.'

Whatever Cromwell's intentions, sentence was passed and recorded in the Newgate register for 21 June 1654:

S' JOHN SOUTHWORTH
pro. *Seminar. Sacerdot.'*
po. se. cul. ca. null. S.'
to be drawne, hanged and quartered.

S' – *suspendatur* – let him be hanged.
Pro. *Seminar. Sacerdot.'* – for being a Seminary Priest
po. se. – *point se* – he puts himself on a jury.
cul. – *culpabilis* – found guilty.
ca. null. – *catella nulla* – no property.
S' – *suspendatur* – let him be hanged.

‘All admired his constancy’

ST JOHN SOUTHWORTH, the last English priest to be executed simply for being a priest, was brought to Tyburn on 28 June 1654. *The Perfect Diurnall,* the record of Parliament’s proceedings, recounts

> This day there was executed at Tyburn nine men and one woman condemned by the session at Old Bailey, whereof one a Jesuit, or as some say, a Secular Romish Priest, who was formerly condemned, pardoned, and banished, but returning hither again was apprehended, and now hanged, drawn and quartered.

Various accounts of onlookers testify to the witness to his faith that John Southworth gave on his last day of earthly life. According to the French Ambassador, ‘two hundred coaches, and a great many people on horseback, who all admired his constancy.’ The Secretary of the Venetian Ambassador recorded what he saw the day after John Southworth’s death:

> Yesterday being appointed for the execution of twelve other criminals, he was led with ignominy to his doom, and before an immense multitude of spectators proclaimed a Papist, a seducer of the people and a disturber of the peace. Then in a

> fashion worse than barbarous, when he was only half dead, the executioner cut out his heart and entrails and threw them into a fire kindled for the purpose, the body being quartered, one for each of the quarters of the city. Such is the inhuman cruelty used towards the English Catholic religious. When discovered they can hope for no pardon… To the last he displayed the greatest cheerfulness, determination and constancy, and at the point of death he boldly thanked the Almighty for permitting him to die for his faith, declaring that on no other account did he deserve his sentence, as he had never offended the state or its government. His extreme firmness and courage taken with his uniformly virtuous life have won him tears and sympathy even of the Protestants and he certainly deserves to be enrolled among the martyrs of the Catholic faith, which gains ground daily owing to the confusion of other creeds.

Bishop Challoner, in his *Memoirs of Missionary Priests*, quoted another eyewitness of the execution:

> As I arrived here I was invited to be a spectator for the martyrdom of Mr. Southworth an ancient secular priest. He had formerly been condemned and reprieved in Lancashire. At his execution, though it was a stormy and rainy day, there came thousands of people, with a great number of coaches and horsemen. He made a speech at the gallows, which I send you with these, according to a copy I had from one of the same profession, who stood under the gallows. The large particulars I have not as yet, nor

seek to send, on confidence you will have them from better hands. Priests fly hence apace, as presaging a greater storm. There are others in hold, and search made after more. All are in fears and suspense, not knowing where to dispose themselves, the times are so hard … There were five coiners hanged, drawn and quartered with Mr. Southworth. He was clothed in a priest's gown, and had a four-cornered cap.

AN ENGRAVING THAT DEPICTS A MARTYR BEING DRAGGED ON A HURDLE TO THE PLACE OF HIS DEATH BEFORE BEING HANGED, DRAWN AND QUARTERED

As was the custom, the condemned man was permitted to make an address to the crowds should he so wish. John Southworth made such a speech which has come down to us in five closely similar versions, indicating that they probably come from one source. It is more than likely that this source may have been a disguised priest who would have positioned himself near the scaffold in order to give John Southworth Absolution at the last. This speech of Southworth is the only address of his that is extant:

> Good people, I was born in Lancashire. This is the third time I have been apprehended, and now being to die, I would gladly witness and profess openly my faith for which I suffer. And though my time be short, yet what I shall be deficient in words I hope I shall supply with my blood, which I will most willingly spend to the last drop for my faith. Neither my intent in coming into England, nor practice in England, was to act anything against the secular government. Hither I was sent by my lawful superiors to teach Christ's faith, not to meddle with any temporal affairs. Christ sent His apostles; His apostles their successors; and their successors me. I did what I was commanded by them, who had power to command me, being ever taught that I ought to obey them in matters ecclesiastical, and my temporal governors in business only temporal. I never acted nor thought any hurt against the present Protector. I had only a care to do my own obligation and discharge my own duty in saving my own and other men's souls. This, and only this, according to my poor abilities I laboured to perform. I had

commission to do it from him to whom our Saviour in his predecessor St Peter gave power to send others to propagate His faith. This is that for which I die, O holy cause! And not for any treason against the laws. My faith and obedience to my superiors is all the treason charged against me; nay, I die for Christ's law, which no human law, by whomsoever made, ought to withstand or contradict. The law of Christ commanded me to obey these superiors and this Church, saying, whoever hears them hears Himself. This Church, these superiors of it I obeyed, and for obeying, die. This lesson I have heretofore in my lifetime desired to learn; this lesson I come here to put in practice by dying, being taught it by our Blessed Saviour, both by precept and example. Himself said: "He that will be My disciple, let him take up his cross and follow Me." Himself exemplary, practised what He had recommended to others. To follow His holy doctrine and imitate His holy death, I willingly suffer at present; this gallows (*looking up)* I look on as His cross, which I gladly take to follow my dear Saviour. My faith is my crime, the performance of my duty the occasion of my condemnation. I confess I am a great sinner; against God I have offended, but am innocent of any sin against man, I mean the Commonwealth and the present Government. How justly then I die, let them look to who have condemned me. It is sufficient for me that it is God's will; I plead not for myself (I came hither to suffer) but for you poor persecuted Catholics whom I leave behind me. Heretofore liberty of conscience was pretended as a cause of war; and it was held a reasonable proposition that

> all the natives should enjoy it, who should be found to behave themselves as obedient and true subjects. This being so, why should their conscientious acting and governing themselves, according to the faith received from their ancestors, involve them more than all the rest in an universal guilt? – which conscientiousness is the very reason that clears others and renders them innocent. It has pleased God to take the sword out of the King's hand and put it in the Protector's. Let him remember that he is to administer justice indifferently and without exception of persons. For there is no exception of persons with God whom we ought to resemble. If any Catholics work against the present Government, let them suffer; but why should all the rest who are guiltless (unless conscience be their guilt) be made partakers in a promiscuous punishment with the greatest malefactors? The first rebellion was of the angels; the guilty were cast into hell, the innocent remained partakers of the heavenly blessings.

The account of the speech, as given by Challoner, continues:

> Here being interrupted by some officers desiring him to make haste, he requested all present that were Catholics to pray for him and with him. Which done, with hands raised up to heaven and eyes (after a short prayer in silence) gently shut, thus devoutly demeaned, he expected the time of his execution, which immediately followed, and which he suffered with an unmoved quietness, delivering his soul most blessedly into the hands of his most loving God, who died for him and for whose sake he died.

The martyrdom had a particular effect on one witness, William Carlos (or Carles), who was a royalist soldier, twenty-three years old. He recorded, 'on witnessing the execution of the most blessed martyr, Mr Southwell [sic], I resolved to seek Rome, in order, as far as in me lies, to render some service, however unworthy, to Holy Church.' Less than three months later, on 9 September 1654, Carlos entered the English College, Rome. He subsequently became a Jesuit and returned to England to serve the mission at Kelvedon, Essex, until his death in 1679.

Douai's Treasure

WHEN REPORTING John Southworth's death, the Venetian Secretary had been correct in assuming that the four quarters of the martyr's body were to be taken for public display to each of the quarters of London. This was the normal procedure, but in the case of John Southworth's remains this did not happen. It was not unknown for the law to be circumvented, for a price, thus enabling family and friends to recover the body for a Christian burial. For forty shillings, John Southworth's body was handed over to the Spanish Ambassador, Don Fluento de Cardenas, who in turn passed it on to, in all probability, the Howard family. According to the Dominican historian, Godfrey Anstruther,

> It is probable that Fr Philip Howard was in London for the execution of Fr Middleton's fellow-prisoner John Southworth on 28 June. Indeed it is probable that it was he who was responsible for having the body embalmed and transported to Douai… The eldest brother was a helpless imbecile at Padua, the second, Henry, was also on the continent, and the others were still in their teens. Hence there appears to be no other claimant for the honour except the young Dominican.

The body was immediately carefully embalmed by one James Clark before being taken to the Spanish Embassy for safekeeping, until such a time arose that it would have been possible to smuggle the martyr's remains out of the country. It was not until a year later that this was achieved, the remains probably having been held in the Embassy Chapel.

On 5 June 1655, shortly after Southworth's remains had arrived at the English College, Douai, Dr George Leyburn, the President, wrote to the Cardinal Protector, Francesco Barberini, stating that the body, embalmed with precious aromatic spices, had been sent by two English Catholics of high rank. In a further letter written that September Leyburn noted that the remains had not been exposed for veneration, although it seems that the head, resting on a cushion and crowned with a wreath of flowers, was left visible. The arrival of the relics had an immediate effect on the local community of Douai:

> Such is the devotion of the people of Douai and their seemingly inborn attraction toward Christ's holy heroes who have sealed their Catholic and Apostolic faith with their blood, that constantly, day by day, they are kneeling at the tomb, pouring out their prayers.

This devotion was more than matched by that of the students who, during the year following the arrival of the martyr's body, witnessed what they believed to be the miraculous cure of the fifteen year old Francis Howard through the intercession of the martyr.

As Thomas Progers, the Professor of Divinity, recorded:

> About the beginning of last vacation he fell sick of a quartan ague in his first day's journey towards Brussels and other parts which he desired to see. It continued with him all his journey and return till within these three weeks, when (seeing him brought very weak) Mr President thought to send him home, for his own native air, and behold on a sudden he is taken with a most violent and malignant fever which, after two days brought him to a frenzy; the doctor feared him very much from the beginning and found him every day worse than other. So that after five days two more were called; after some visits, with small hopes, they all one night deserted him, saying jointly he would infallibly die before morning (and they were held for the learnedest and greatest practitioners of the university) and indeed the signs were as mortal as could be in a dying man. He had not slept in four or five days, and raved as long; his pulse was convulsive; his tongue very black, dry, rough and shrunk; his countenance and eyes (in the estimation of all that beheld him) of a man agonising, so the doctor told the President, "There is not the least hope". All were very sad at this sentence, but especially Mr President as being the common and tender father of all and of this in particular being of a great family, of an excellent disposition, a pretty scholar, generally beloved, very regular, discreet, virtuous, etc.; briefly such an one as we had placed in him no small part of the hopes of this house. The President therefore, much troubled and disconsolate, bethought himself it was

this youth's brother sent us our Blessed Martyr's body, and presently, directing his devotion to the Martyr, fell upon his knees and prayed heartily as you may be sure, promising with all, if he but lived till morning he would carry a little crown of flowers which we keep over the Martyr's head, to him. The youth began to mend beyond all hopes and expectations that night. Next morning the crown was brought and a cushion which lies under the Martyr's head was laid under his. He grew better every day since and is now got up these two days to our great admiration and comfort, and to the greater glory of God in His Saints and in this His Blessed Martyr. The doctors that night they left him, thinking no more to see him, had given order none should come near him but who needs must, and those to keep constantly a good fire and when he was dead (which they made no question would be in very few hours) to open all windows and doors, wash and air all the clothes about him, so pernicious they deemed the disease. The doctor called next morning (for they had never stirred of themselves), wondered little less than if a man had been raised from the dead, and seeing the alteration, one of them did assure the President that neither nature in him nor art in them had wrought this change, to which his sentence I cannot see anything which can be reasonably objected. So though I never found myself an easy proclaimer of miracles upon slight grounds, but rather contrary, yet truly, for a miraculous recovery of a man only not quite dead, I know not what the nicest believer can require more in prudence. So I believe it, though a Thomas too.

Some years later Dr Edward Paston, President of Douai from 1688 until 1714, related of the miracle that

> This happened in Doway [sic] College in the year 1656. Dr. George Leyburn was then President of this our College in Doway. The young man thus strangely cured was Mr. Francis Howard, brother to the Duke of Norfolk… The Martyr is Mr John Southworth whose body lies by St Augustine's altar, and was then in a little room which now, in this present year 1701, is the Church porch. The author of this relation is Mr Thomas Progers who was at that time Professor of Divinity. I was then about fifteen years of age, and have only a confused memory of what happened in those days but remember somewhat of it.

That the most illustrious miracle worked through the intercession of John Southworth was for the benefit of a younger brother of the one who had taken so much trouble to secure the martyr's relics, seems most fitting. In due course Francis Howard became a Dominican, like his brother Philip, but although he became a deacon, various illnesses and attacks of scruples prevented his ordination to the priesthood. He died aged 45.

It is not clearly recorded how John Southworth's body was kept during its years at Douai. It seems to have first rested in a small room and later found a resting place near the altar of St Augustine, on the gospel side of the chapel. In 1701 one writer records that the body was kept 'by St Augustine's altar', and this is supported by Challoner, writing in the

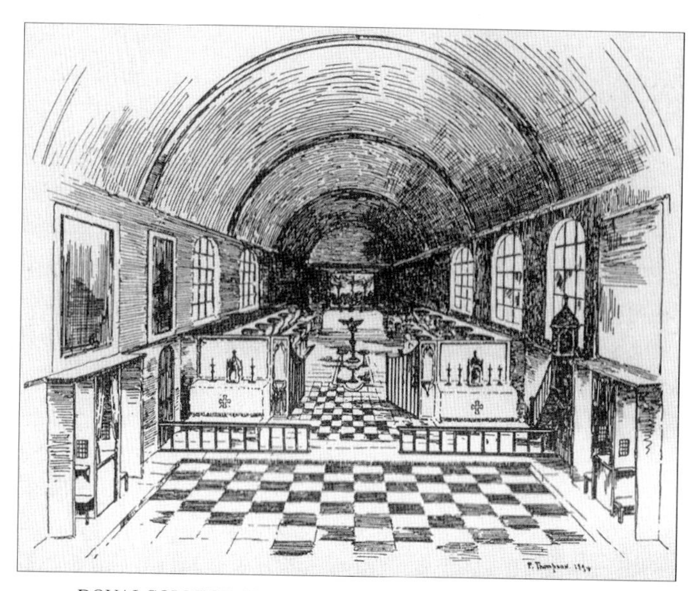

DOUAI COLLEGE CHAPEL IN THE EIGHTEENTH CENTURY

early 1740s. Certainly the College authorities did not wish to pre-empt in any manner the final decision of the Pope as to the sanctity of Southworth and so there was no 'shrine' or any attempt to encourage an excessive *cultus*. Providentially, a leaden shell was provided for the body which enabled its safe concealment and survival during the revolution.

The ensuing chaos of the French Revolution necessitated the secret burial of all that the College most treasured. Bishop Douglass (Vicar Apostolic of the London District 1790–1812) left notes concerning the exact locations of all the important buried treasures, noting that Southworth's body was 'in the Kilns exactly in the middle – six feet deep.' A further document left by Fr Thomas Stout, who was General Prefect of the College in 1793 and probably responsible for concealing the College's principal relics, gives a plan of the area of the kilns, marking the burial site clearly. An unsubstantiated record notes that the burial was carried out on 4 May 1793.

After the closure of the college as an ecclesiastical establishment the buildings took on various uses and smaller out buildings were added, while other structures were demolished. Consequently the careful plans and notes regarding the burial of the College treasures made less and less sense. Given the political turmoil in France and the preoccupation of establishing sufficient provision for the training of priests in England, it is unsurprising that no real attempt was made to retrieve the 'Douai Treasure' until May 1863. Mgr Canon Francis Searle, Cardinal Wiseman's secretary, made careful plans, with the permission of the Emperor Napoleon III, to recover the relics. On 18 May digging commenced and the following day a decayed wooden box containing a collection of the College's silver was discovered.

THE FORMER ENGLISH COLLEGE, DOUAI,
SHORTLY BEFORE ITS DEMOLITION

Nothing further was found and, being unable to excavate the whole site, the searchers then resorted to probe the ground with a long sharp-pointed iron rod. Such a device was hardly subtle, having to be hammered into the ground. The search party would never have known if they had hit the lead coffin of John Southworth as the rod would – and in fact probably did – penetrate the lead with great ease. The relics remained in the ground, undiscovered.

With the failure of the 1863 search, all hope of finding Southworth's remains seems to have been comprehensively dashed. As Bernard Ward recorded in his *History of St Edmund's College* (1893),

> The body of the Ven. John Southworth, the martyr, was also one of the Douai treasures… No trace was discovered by Mgr Searle of this or any other of the relics. Even if he had known exactly where to look – and it seems that, owing to changes in the internal structure, there was in some cases considerable difficulty in identifying the precise spot – it is more than doubtful whether anything would have been left of them after seventy-five years under ground.

If it had not been for proposals made in 1923 for the redevelopment of part of the town of Douai where the College stood, it is not at all impossible that the relics of St John Southworth might have been lost forever. The scheme involved the demolition of some of the old College buildings that had been used as barracks, so that a new road could run diagonally across the site from the centre of the town to the railway station. The land on one side of the road was to be levelled and left as an open space, whilst the land on the other side was to be sold for the use of private developers. The great Benedictine historian, Fr Bede Camm, became aware of the impending work and notified Cardinal Francis Bourne, Archbishop of Westminster and President of St Edmund's College, Ware, one of the successors of Douai. The Cardinal was quick in alerting friends and the authorities in Douai, making them aware that some of the College treasures might come to light during the town redevelopment.

It was only in 1926, however, that work on the project got under way and by September of that year demolition work on the site was completed. The local historical society, *Les Amis de Douai*, under the Presidency of M.F. de Bailliencourt, kept a watchful eye on proceedings. Bailliencourt had already attempted to preserve the College chapel from demolition by trying to raise funds in England for its preservation. This scheme was not successful although Bailliencourt and *Les Amis* were not to lose interest in the site.

The treasure was known to be contained in three boxes: the first contained the relics of St Thomas of Canterbury and St Charles Borromeo; the second contained relics of the martyrs, and the third box held the precious Church plate. *Les Amis* were not looking for the whole body of a martyr. Once the old buildings had been razed to the ground, Bailliencourt employed M. Depreux and the Abbé Bouly, two metal-diviners, to search the site, but with no success.

At about the same time, Baillencourt informed the Director of Public Property and the Mayor of Douai of what he hoped might be discovered beneath the rubble of the college.

It was some months after the new road had been completed that the land lying to the north-west was divided up and sold. The area on which the College had stood was bought by M. Marcoux who had the area levelled. Providentially there was one plot that required a cellar to be constructed and it was during the necessary excavations for this that, on the morning of 15 July 1926, the workmen unearthed a leaden coffin-like shell about five feet below the level of the new road. The coffin was about five feet eight inches in length and was moulded in the shape of the body that lay within, its head positioned towards the south-east. Amidst the driving rain of the day of excavations, two holes were observed in the casket – one, approximately one and a half inches in diameter, in the upper part of the coffin near its centre, the other being a small hole at the head, caused by the pickaxe of the workmen who made the discovery. The workmen, hoping that treasure lay within, were fortunately prevented from opening the coffin, which was quickly taken to the local morgue.

Here the surface of the coffin was first carefully cleaned in the hope that some form of inscription might identify the remains contained within. No inscription or other means of identification being discovered on the outside of the coffin, the attendants at the morgue proceeded to carefully open the lead shell. Inside they discovered a body tightly wrapped in linen bands, the head inclined a little towards the right shoulder.

The next day brought a further discovery. Approximately eight feet from where the coffin had been discovered, the remains of a wooden box were found. It had been wrapped around with lead in the hope that this would prevent the wood from rotting and thus it had been able to preserve its precious contents. Unlike the coffin, the lead had not been strong enough to withstand the passage of time – the wooden box was rotten and had fallen to pieces. Unsupervised, the workmen kept what they thought might be of some interest – this was in fact pieces of the scarlet biretta of St Charles Borromeo – and they discarded what they thought a piece of mere packing material, 'a piece of rough hairy material like a portion of carpet,' – undoubtedly this was part of the hair shirt of St Thomas. The former relic had been given to Douai College by the Revd Thomas Harley in 1616, this priest having received it from the Revd Hugh Griffen of Cambrai. He had, in turn, received it from the very man in whose arms the saintly Archbishop of Milan had died, Dr Owen Lewis, Borromeo's Vicar General and future Bishop of Cassano. Despite desperate searching once the authorities had been alerted to the workmen's error, the relic of St Thomas was never recovered. Nor were the boxes containing the other relics and College plate.

Beneath the pieces of Borromeo's biretta was found a square of embroidery that once may have been either a pall or a burse. Almost certainly it too was a relic but we have no evidence to even suggest in what manner it might be so. Due to the biretta and the piece of embroidered cloth being pressed together for so long, one of the pieces of the biretta bears the imprint of the cloth's embroidery, the IHS monogram set within the sun in its glory.

BIRETTA OF CHARLES BORROMEO

On 18 July Dr Leclercq, the Director of the Institute of Legal Medicine at Lille, carried out an inspection of the body observing that

> The wrappings, which had been submitted to some preservative process, were of very strong linen, and

were only removed with difficulty, disclosing the body of a man. The water that had penetrated through the hole in the shell had done much damage to the chest and stomach, which had both fallen apart: on the whole, however, the body had kept its general form quite well. The head in particular was found to be in a good state of preservation; the skin of the face had taken on a coppery tint, and there was a slight moustache *à la Richelieu* of chestnut colour; the orbs of the eyes were empty and the ears had been severed. The crown of the head had been carefully sawn off and the brain entirely removed; in the cavity were wads of embalming material. The head was found to be sewn to the trunk by careful stitching at the neck. The thoracic and abdominal viscera had been removed and the voids filled with preservative material. Both hands had been taken off at the wrists. There were incisions down the inside of the forearms, made for the purpose of embalmment, and these were carefully sewn. There were similar incisions and stitches on other parts of the body.

Of the missing members, hands, ears and crown of the head, there was no trace in the coffin, nor did a painstaking search reveal any sign of a document or object of any kind which might have given a clue to the identity of the body or the date of its burial.

News of the discoveries spread quickly, the imaginations of various reporters leading to increasingly bizarre and sensational reports. In the days following the removal of the lead coffin it was reported in some local papers that perhaps the remains of a crusader had been found. Another paper suggested that Douai had its own Tutankhamen, whilst an American paper reported that the body was none other than that of St Thomas Becket.

Where the leaden casket had been punctured there were clear signs of the decomposition of the body, yet the head and the left forearm were in excellent condition. In order to ensure their conservation, these parts were removed and taken to Lille for further treatment. The flesh on the legs was also noticed to have been in good condition.

On Thursday 28 July, Fr Albert Bertrand Purdie *(left)*, a Westminster priest and Assistant Headmaster at St Edmund's College, arrived in Douai, having been sent by Cardinal Bourne. Up until this point, M. de Bailliencourt had assumed that the body that had been discovered was that of Fr Richard Southworth, a former Vice Rector of the College. A principal task for Fr Purdie was to discover, with as much certainty as possible, the identity of the body which he believed to be that of the martyred John Southworth. Together with Dr Leclercq, Fr Purdie examined the head. At this stage there seemed to be a marked discrepancy between the age at which John Southworth is thought to have died – sixty-two – and the appearance of the head. Dr Leclercq pointed to the good condition of the teeth, the lack of any grey or white hair and the complete absence of any wrinkles on the forehead as evidence that the body was that of a man in his early fifties when he died. Two years later Dr Leclercq revised his opinion about this, concurring that the body might indeed have been that of a man in his early sixties.

A further examination process involved researching the manner in which the body had been embalmed. This was undertaken by M.E. Leclair who declared that the original embalmer, James Clark, had carefully followed the method of Philbert Guybert as set out in his work *Les Oeuvres du médecin charitable* of 1629. With these initial investigations completed, Fr Purdie returned to England to fetch a relic of John Southworth that was held at Westminster Cathedral which, according to an attached note, was a 'bone taken of ye neck of Mr. Southworth.' Meanwhile the exhumed body was taken to Lille where, under the direction of M. Theodore, the Director of the *Palais des Beaux Arts* at Lille, the body was to be carefully and thoroughly dried and new conservation methods applied.

On 4 August Fr Purdie arrived once more in Douai and, with M. de Bailliencourt, M. Theodore and M. Leclair, he once again examined the body, hoping that the relic that he had brought from Westminster would 'settle the question of identity beyond all dispute.' But it would not, at least not immediately, for the left clavicle was still present in the body. M. Leclair pointed out that it was also most unlikely that the original embalmer would have removed such an important bone from the body in

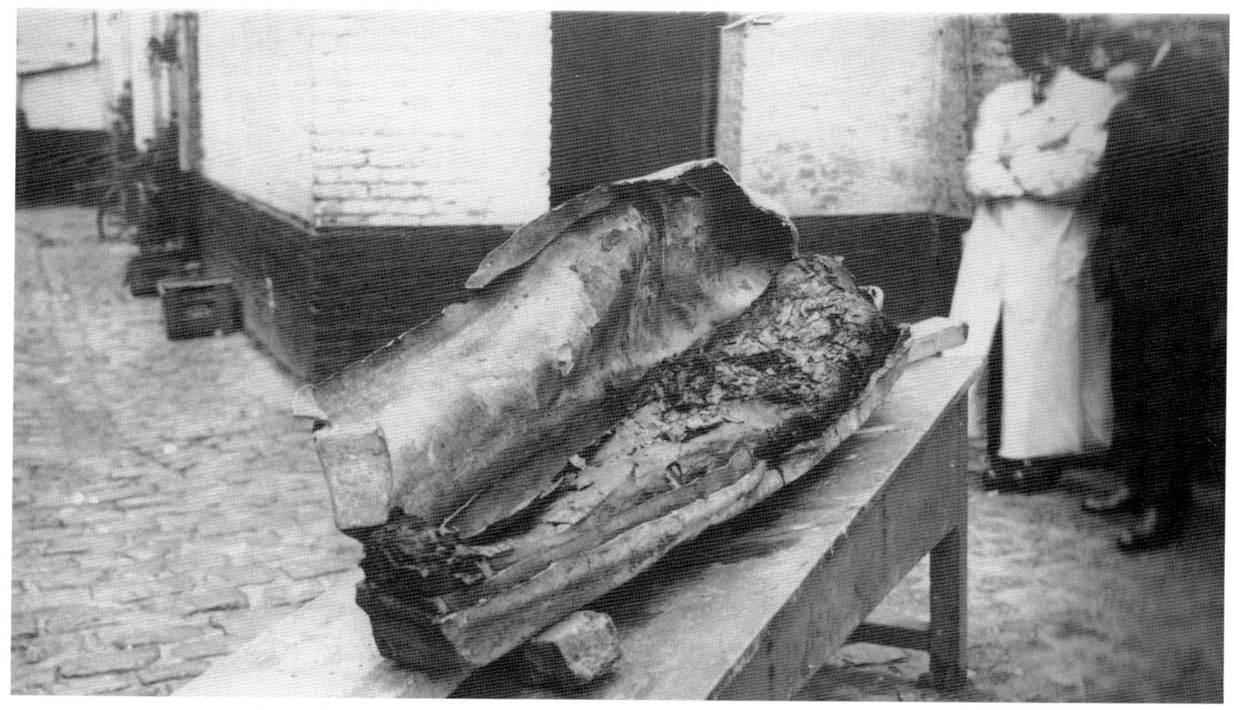

THE LEADEN SHELL CONTAINING THE BODY OF ST JOHN SOUTHWORTH

order to give it to a friend. Leclair, however, had discovered that there was 'a deep transversal cut through the neck vertebrae and part of the vertebrae of the thorax. Some parts of the neck vertebrae were missing, and perhaps it was a loose fragment, "a bone out of the neck," that Mr Clark, in cleaning and embalming the body, had given as a relic to his friend.'

These impressions of Leclair were confirmed by the negatives of X-ray photographs that were taken shortly after the discovery of the remains. As Purdie related, these pictures also proved beyond all doubt that

> the body had been quartered. The head had been cut off probably with an axe or chopper, and both legs had been similarly severed: there was a violent cut through the dorsal vertebrae, and the pelvis was irregularly broken in two: the hip joints were not disturbed. It was easy to see where the quarters had been sewn together by Mr James Clark.

With regards the clavicle that was held at Westminster Cathedral, it would seem that the bone and the note that was with it were simply mismatched. A catalogue of the Relics of the English Martyrs drawn up by Dom Ethelbert Horne lists under the name Southworth 'a small bone probably of this martyr', thus demonstrating that there had always been a certain amount of doubt as to the bone's provenance.

Although there were a great number of clues that pointed to the body being that of Southworth, some form of positive identification was still needed. This came over a year later when Fr Marron, a Benedictine at Douai Abbey, contacted Fr Purdie to say that his community had in their archives copies of the documents used by the 1863 Commission. Amongst these was Fr Stout's plan of where the martyr's body had been buried, together with the other treasures of the College. These plans proved beyond all doubt that the body discovered was indeed that of John Southworth.

Purdie goes on to relate,

> The remains of the martyr rested at Lille for nearly five months, and during that time, no pains nor expense were spared to secure their continued preservation and to restore the body as near as possible to the condition in which it left the hands of James Clark and to the appearance it must have had when it first lay exposed in the little chapel at Douai College. In the meantime the necessary formalities were exchanged between the Cardinal Archbishop of Westminster, the French *Affaires Étrangères* and our own Foreign Office, and at last permission was granted to transfer the remains to England.
>
> On December 20, 1927, the body of Blessed John Southworth was handed over to me as the representative of the Cardinal by the French authorities – intact except for the right forearm and the left clavicle, which at the earnest prayer of the Archbishop of Cambrai were left at Douai as precious memorials of the great English College

> which for three hundred years was an ornament of hospitable Flanders and a glory of the Faith throughout the Catholic world…
>
> I travelled by rail to Calais and crossed by the passenger-boat, with none on board conscious of the sacred burden: from Dover I proceeded by road to London and thence to St Edmund's College, Ware, which with Ushaw is the lineal descendant of Douai on English soil.

For the following three years the body of John Southworth – the only martyr of the Reformation whose mortal remains have come down to us in such substantial form – rested in the Douai Room at St Edmund's, Ware.

The martyr's face caused a great impact, especially after a portrait was drawn by John Trinick, based on a photograph taken at the time of the discovery. Many years later, in a letter written to the Cathedral Administrator, Fr Purdie reminisced: 'when I first saw the body at Douai the face looked very restful (not at all horrific) and I detected the faint glimmer of a smile, as of one well content.'

The return to Westminster

WHILE HIS BODY was resting at St Edmund's College, Southworth was included among the 136 English Martyrs beatified by Pope Pius XI. Even before Southworth's death the first steps had been taken to have some of the English martyrs recognised by the Church for their heroic witness but, due to the on-going persecution and suppression of the Church in Britain, no real progress could be made until after the restoration of the Hierarchy in 1850. On 9 December 1886, Pope Leo XIII introduced the cause of 254 English martyrs. Only weeks later, on 29 December 1886 – the Feast of St Thomas of Canterbury – the Pope confirmed the cult of 54 of these martyrs by special decree, confirming the cult of a further nine on 13 May 1895.

On 8 December 1929, the seventy-fifth anniversary of the proclamation of the Dogma of the Immaculate Conception, the beatification of the 136 English martyrs, John Southworth among them, was approved by the pope. It was a momentous year, also marking the hundredth anniversary of the Catholic Emancipation Act and the fiftieth anniversary of the Holy Father's priestly ordination. With the Apostolic Letter *Atrocissima tormenta passi* of 15 December 1929, Pope Pius beatified the English Martyrs and the following week, on 22 December, honoured the Scottish martyr, John Ogilvy, in a similar way. *The Tablet* reported the ceremonies:

> On 15th December, 1929, the solemn ceremony of Beatification took place in St Peter's in the presence of a vast multitude. The wonderful Basilica, brilliantly illuminated, wears a majesty on these occasions, which enhances the character of the solemnity, and the vast throng filling it gives some idea of its immensity. The first Mass in honour of the new Beatified Martyrs was celebrated with all the splendour of ceremony and music for which St Peter's is famous.
>
> After Mass the Holy Father received a deputation from the Catholic Union of Great Britain, introduced by His Eminence Cardinal Bourne. In the absence of the Union's President, Lord FitzAlan, through ill health, it fell to the Earl of Denbigh to read the address to the Sovereign Pontiff in which he recalled that the Union was established to uphold Papal sovereignty.
>
> In the afternoon the Holy Father came to venerate the relics of the one hundred and thirty-six newly beatified martyrs. Thousands of English pilgrims were present in St Peter's for this historic occasion. They watched with a sense of awe and excitement as the Holy Father, dressed in his traditional white, was borne aloft up the centre of the great nave. Naturally one's mind went back to those heroic figures whose relics the Vicar of Christ had come to

venerate. What a contrast between the triumphant enthusiasm of this day and their execution when most were dragged through the muddy streets to their Calvary, where the tall gibbet and the hangman's rope awaited them. The names of their executioners and persecutors are forgotten, buried in oblivion; but God's saints are held in everlasting remembrance, and this is the day of their triumph.

After this brief ceremony all those present prepared to venerate Our Blessed Lord in the monstrance; an act of veneration for which the Martyrs had been willing to give their lives as they consecrated the Sacred Host during Holy Mass in secret chapels throughout England. After Benediction of the Blessed Sacrament the Holy Father was once again carried in his sedatorial chair back along the nave blessing the faithful on his right and left as he went. The great day was nearly over; one which will never fade from the memory of those privileged to take part in it.

In St Peter's Basilica, Pope Pius XI spoke of the martyrs' witness:

Our first words are those of gratitude to the Divine Goodness which has brought another superhuman joy by a spectacle that is both grand and intensely appealing. We see before our eyes the new array of Beatified Martyrs from England and Scotland. We hail them not only in the name of their Church and country, but on behalf of the whole Church, rejoicing as we behold them ascend to the honours of the altar in the sight of the King of Martyrs. They all come as children of Christ, as belonging to that people of election which is the Church, where all are equally called to sanctity and where each one can climb the supreme heights of heroism and holiness. The new martyrs remind us that we are indeed the children of the saints, capable if need be to make the supreme sacrifice.

We declare that these martyrs were not merely heroes of the Church in that sense which we may term generic, but the martyrs of this Roman Church whose secret infallibility which is founded upon the rock of Peter, upon Papal authority, a Divine Disposition, which dominating history has given a Roman character to the Church. Therefore these new martyrs are martyrs of the Papacy, of the Roman Church, in a word, our martyrs. We would then give expression to the great and particular joy we feel in being able to render the highest recompense to them which the Goodness of God has placed in our hands through the power of the Keys.

Like the blood of the first Christians, the heroic sacrifice of these new English and Scottish martyrs avails to maintain the sacred fire of Truth, Fidelity to the Church, and the Vicar of Jesus Christ, the Roman Pope. The Beatification of these holy men and women who gave their lives so readily for the Faith gladdens our heart as it did the King of Martyrs in His prayer on the eve of His sacrifice, which not only consoled Him in the hour of sadness,

> but consoled too, by the promised advent of the one sheep-fold beneath the One Shepherd.

The joy following the beatification of the English martyrs was shared in England. At Westminster Cathedral a solemn *Te Deum* was sung at Benediction after news of the beatification was confirmed by telegram. The faithful flocked to a small shrine that had been erected in St George's Chapel. At St Edmund's, where the body of Blessed John Southworth rested, there was similar jubilation:

> When the Beatification was an accomplished fact, the whole College went in procession on Sunday evening to the little Douai Oratory in the main building, chanting on the way the Psalms of the Office of a Martyr. The red ribbon that sealed the door was cut, and presently the casket was carried out, borne on the shoulders of six stoled deacons. The long procession, which now carried lighted tapers and extended down each side of President's Gallery, broke out into the impressive strains of the hymn, "Martyrs of England, standing on high," as the body was taken along the great ambulacrum to the College chapel. When the South door was reached, "Faith of our Fathers" was sung with a vigour and animation that were truly thrilling. The procession passed slowly through the ante-Chapel in front of Pugin's beautiful rood-screen, and the casket was deposited near the Lady Altar. It was draped with a red pall, and over the head was placed a beautiful crown of flowers, reminiscent of the old Douai days, when according to a contemporary

account the body of the Martyr lay exposed in "a little room" and had a "croune of flowers" upon the head.

At each corner stood handsome candlesticks, and each candle bore a small circlet of ribbon carrying the Douai colours – red, fringed with alternate squares of black and gold. The celebrant and his assistants stood by the side of the casket, and when masters and students had filled the ante-chapel the *Te Deum* was intoned and sung to the well-known Gregorian setting. A short prayer followed, and then the procession, to the jubilant chant of "God bless our Pope," proceeded to the choir of the Chapel where Solemn Benediction was given.

THE CASKET CONTAINING THE BODY OF BLESSED JOHN SOUTHWORTH RESTING AT ST EDMUND'S, WARE

As the President of the College, Mgr Myers, was away in Rome, the College celebration was presided over by the headmaster, Fr Purdie, who had been so intimately involved in the identification of the relics and had written a biography of the martyr.

With his beatification, the path was cleared for the solemn translation of Blessed John Southworth's body to Westminster Cathedral. On 30 April 1930, which was the Wednesday of Low Week, his relics were brought firstly to the convent in Tyburn, yards away from the site of his execution. Then, at 11.30am, Blessed John Southworth was taken to the Cathedral. The body was first placed in the Cathedral Hall. This had been set up as a chapel, the Cardinal's vestments set out on an altar placed against the back wall. In the centre, between two rows of benches and surrounded by four candlesticks, a dais covered in red baize supported the reliquary that was to receive the beatus' body.

In the Cathedral a Triduum commenced with Solemn Mass at 10.30am on Thursday 1 May. At 3.15pm Vespers was sung, after which the translation of the relics to the Chapel of St George and the English Martyrs took place. One observer, Evelyn Thomas, wrote that

> as we watched from a window directly opposite the thought came again and again: "Are we in Protestant England or have we gone back to pre-Reformation days?" and as the procession passed we realised that this solemn pageant was an actual historical event, the first occasion of the enshrining of a saint in

THE TRANSLATION OF THE RELICS OF BLESSED JOHN SOUTHWORTH, 1ST MAY 1930

> London since the Reformation…The solemn tolling of the bell heralded the procession, which was headed by the men of the Blessed Sacrament Guild, in scarlet habits, followed by the choir, the clergy and the Cathedral Chapter, chanting the Psalms from the Vespers of a Martyr. In the midst was the martyr, in his crystal casket, veiled in white, borne by six *[sic]* priests. As he passed, the Convent children sank on their knees, and each little head was reverently bowed.

One of the eight priests carrying the casket was Fr Purdie. In front, were coped bishops in gold mitres and, behind, Cardinal Bourne wearing a precious mitre and holding his crosier. Having entered the Cathedral, the procession headed for St George's Chapel, where the sacred relics were incensed and the prescribed prayers said. With the translation completed, the Cardinal presided at Benediction and the singing of the *Te Deum*. Crowds continued to venerate the relics for the rest of the day, touching their rosaries and scapulars to the casket. A further service was held in the evening, at which the Abbot of Downside preached.

Such was the interest in the arrival of the relics, that it was decided they would remain exposed for a month. At the end of May 1930 the martyr's casket was covered by a teak outer case with a glass window in the side fitted with red silk curtains, enabling Blessed John Southworth's body to be seen by the faithful on less solemn occasions when the outer casing was not removed. It was intended that this cover should be temporary, the *Cathedral Chronicle* declaring that 'a richer permanent one is in contemplation as soon as sufficient offerings are received for the purpose.'

THE SHRINE OF BLESSED JOHN SOUTHWORTH
AS SEEN SHORTLY AFTER HIS REMAINS WERE TRANSLATED TO
WESTMINSTER CATHEDRAL

At the time of the translation, the Chapel of St George and the English Martyrs was largely undecorated. The Eric Gill altarpiece and the sculpted relief of St George were yet to be commissioned. Inspired by the arrival of the relics, new work on the chapel was completed in 1930, including the marble floor and the grille of polished bronze that separates the chapel from the north aisle of the Cathedral. Incorporated into this fine grille a space was designed to enable the Faithful to kneel and pray before Blessed John Southworth's body, the armrest provided being of rosewood, inlaid with ivory, padouk and ebony. Shortly afterwards a bronze and enamel box, in which petitions could be left at the shrine, was designed and installed by the new grille. At either end of the chapel were hung the great paintings that were used in St Peter's Basilica on the day of the beatification.

‘Our Precious Relics’

IN THE years after the beatification, one of the Cathedral Chaplains, Fr James Hathway, was appointed to record and publish favours received through the martyr. Accounts of the beatus’ intercession were regularly published in the *Westminster Cathedral Chronicle* between 1931 and 1936. They included thanksgiving for renewed health, financial assistance and employment found:

> My wife was taken ill last month and had to have a day and a night nurse with the doctor coming twice a day… As hope became fainter every day, I determined to make a novena to Blessed John, and for nine days I visited his shrine at the Cathedral; at each visit I recited five decades of the Rosary. On the seventh day, which was my birthday, I asked for a sign, and on that evening the doctor told me after he had seen my wife that for the first time she had taken a step in the right direction. Since that day she has gone on recovering… The doctor, himself a non-Catholic, told my wife it was something above human skill which cured her; he also added that he had never seen a patient so ill as she had been, and recover. (1933)

A burst artery caused much pain when M. B. walked, was eased by the application of a rosary that had been laid on the shrine of Blessed John. Likewise muscular rheumatism. (1931)

I prayed to Blessed John at his tomb and offered Holy Mass and Communion all last week, and lo! After fruitless searching, I found a very nice flat… Moreover, my landlord, a very fierce Mexican, suddenly thawed and allowed me to sublet, and move next Tuesday. I shall now therefore be able to start my little daughter on (her hospital) treatment at once, thanks to Blessed John. (1934)

In a convent, a misunderstanding was put right in a most extraordinary way through the intercession of Blessed John. (1932)

From Stockholm. Thanksgiving for very special favour received. (1933)

In 1931 the martyr was celebrated in a play written by Miss Kirchberger and performed by the 'Blessed John Southworth Girl's Club', recalling 'typical episodes from the blessed martyr's pastorate, apprehension, trial and martyrdom' and concluding with 'a photographic lantern picture of the martyr's shrine in the Cathedral.' The same year *A Ballad of Blessed John Southworth* was composed by Miss Enid Dinnis and published by the Manresa Press.

The martyr was further remembered in the Blessed John Southworth Hostel which stood on Vauxhall Bridge Road in the 1930s 'to cater for the needs of working boys between the ages of 14 and 18 years, particularly those who had come from residential schools.' It formed part of the work of the Crusade of Rescue and was administered by the Brothers of the Hospitaller Order of St John of God.

ST GEORGE'S CHAPEL IN 1930 SHOWING THE NEW BRONZE SCREEN AND THE MARBLE FLOOR OF THE CHAPEL

1954 saw the tercentenary of Southworth's martyrdom and on 27 June Cardinal Bernard Griffin sang a Pontifical Mass in his honour, at which Mgr Ronald Knox preached, and after the *Te Deum* a procession was made to the shrine. At the end of the year the Cardinal obtained permission to open the reliquary casket in order to dress the body in contemporary vestments, including a 'four-cornered cap' similar to the one he wore at his execution, and to place a silver mask over the martyr's face.

As the twentieth century progressed the Hierarchy of England and Wales addressed the desire of many Catholics to canonise at least some of the beatified martyrs. Fr Paolo Molinari, the Postulator General of the Society of Jesus and President of the College of Postulators, was given the task of promoting the cause and nominated the English Jesuits Fr Philip Caraman and Fr James Walsh as Assistant Postulators. Due to other commitments, Fr Caraman was eventually replaced by Fr Clement Tigar, also a Jesuit.

From the beatified martyrs of England and Wales forty names were chosen and presented to the Holy See on 1 December 1960. The following year, on 24 May, Blessed John XXIII's Decree *Sanctorum Insula* formally opened the cause of these Forty Martyrs, which included Southworth. Just under nine years later, on 18 May 1970, Pope Paul VI announced the forthcoming canonisation. Having sought the opinion of the Cardinals and other high ranking clerics present, the Holy Father declared:

> We greatly rejoice that unanimously you have asked that these blessed Martyrs of England and Wales be canonised; this is also our desire. It is our intention to enrol them among the saints and to declare them worthy of the honours that the Church attributes to those holy persons who have obtained their heavenly reward. With God's help, we will do this on the twenty-fifth day of October of this year in the Vatican Basilica.

Alongside Blessed John Southworth twelve members of the secular clergy, ten Jesuits, three Benedictines and Carthusians, two Franciscans, one Augustinian and Brigittine and seven members of the laity (including three mothers) were also to be canonised. Pope Paul VI said:

> To all those who are filled with admiration in reading the records of these Forty Holy Martyrs, it is perfectly clear that they are worthy to stand alongside the greatest martyrs of the past; and this not merely because of their fearless faith and marvellous constancy, but by reason of their humility, simplicity and serenity, and above all the spiritual joy and that wondrously radiant love with which they accepted their condemnation and death.

Present in the congregation on 25 October 1970, was Teresa Hynes, a young girl cured of a death-threatening illness thanks to the martyrs' intercession, and relatives of Mrs Matthewman, whose cure from a terminal bone illness had been recognised by the Holy See as the miracle required for canonisation. The music for the occasion was provided not by the

Capella Sistina but the choir of Westminster Cathedral under the direction of Colin Mawby. They sang Byrd's *Mass for Five Voices*, Tallis' *O Sacrum convivium,* Philips' *Ave verum* and Sir Richard Terry's *Vexilla Regis*, as well as leading the hymns 'For all the saints' and 'All people that on earth do dwell' – the first time hymns from the Anglican tradition had been heard at a Papal Mass. *The Times* reported that the choir 'came off with honours in a manful battle with St Peter's notorious acoustic' and Archbishop Bugnini, the architect of many of the liturgical changes following the Second Vatican Council, commented that at the Canonisation 'the revived Papal liturgy reached perhaps its zenith of harmony and meaning.'

Back at the Cathedral, lacking its choir and many of its chaplains, the martyr's shrine was moved to the middle of St George's Chapel, flanked by six brass candlesticks designed by the original Cathedral architect, John Bentley, and recently purchased by the Administrator. The Cathedral *News Sheet* reported that the shrine was 'crowded with pilgrims throughout the day' and that 'one of the Cathedral Chaplains, not content with listening to the canonisation direct from Vatican Radio, had installed a large telescope in his room. Rumour has it that he was intent on making sure that the "binding on earth" really was coincidental with the "binding in Heaven"!'

In early November 1970 a special Triduum of Thanksgiving was held at the Cathedral, during which St John Southworth's body was transferred to the centre of the nave and Masses were celebrated on a portable altar that was placed before the casket. There were special services for 2,000 religious women and nearly 6,000 children and Fr Tigar preached at a solemn concelebrated Mass on the final day. There was also an evening of readings and music, 'The World of John Southworth', at which 'some fine dramatic readings from the writings of the Martyrs themselves and from others of the period, blended smoothly with English sixteenth-century music.'

The following year the Cathedral Administrator, Mgr Canon Francis Bartlett, commissioned a bust of the saint from the sculptor L. Cubbitt Bevis, whose other works included the bronze of St Thomas More on Chelsea Embankment. Small copies were sold in the Cathedral shop.

Devotion to St John Southworth continues to this day. When Blessed John Paul II celebrated Mass at the Cathedral on 28 May 1982, he prayed briefly at the martyr's shrine. In 2007 the Archdiocese of Westminster set up the 'St John Southworth Fund' intended 'to support the work of parishes, organisations or individuals across a range of issues including poverty, old age and infirmity, homelessness and children with disabilities or who are in danger of deprivation.' The Fund recalled the saint's pastoral concern for the marginalised in seventeenth century London. A further sign of recent devotion to St John Southworth was the commissioning by Westminster Cathedral Gift Shop of a new statue of the saint which was created by the artist and sculptor David Cope.

During the 'Year for Priests' (2009-10) Southworth was held up as a model of the Priesthood within the Archdiocese of Westminster and, in 2011, a DVD was produced to promote vocations in schools, featuring pupils from the Douai Martyrs School in Ickenham visiting places connected with St John Southworth.

At the priestly ordinations on 2 July 2011, held at the Cathedral, Archbishop Vincent Nichols said in his homily:

> Shortly, these candidates will prostrate themselves on the floor of the Cathedral, taking up a posture of utter vulnerability, of self-abandonment. They do so as a sign of dying to self, so that Christ may raise them up to a new life in him. They do so in the midst of you, their families, friends and fellow disciples, so that your prayers may strengthen and sustain them. They do so in the company of St John Southworth, whose mortal remains, our precious relics, are there alongside them.
>
> But if we look more closely, we will notice that the saint lies with his face turned upward to God, already full of the glory of the risen Christ. For our part, we prostrate ourselves face downward, knowing that we depend on God's mercy and grace. The one who is dead is now fully alive in God. We who are alive seek to die in Christ so that he may live in us.

The Archbishop went on to note that

> Risking his life, St John Southworth returned again and again to his ministry in the streets around this Cathedral, bringing comfort and love to the poor and the dying, opening for them the sacraments of Christ's love and the Gospel of his mercy. He is a model for every priest. And, like his Master, our saint gave up his life in a painful death, and we, today, treasure his remains and reverence them with love and gratitude.
>
> But, like every priest, St John Southworth wants us to turn our gaze away from him and onto Christ alone. As the Gospel has told us, we are to gaze on the one whom we have pierced. We are to gaze each day on the wounded Christ, for from his wounds flow life and grace and in his wounds we are made whole.

Almighty God,
you made your Church grow
through the missionary zeal and apostolic work
of Saint John Southworth.
By the help of his prayers
give your Church continued growth
in holiness and faith.
Grant this through our Lord Jesus Christ, your Son,
who lives and reigns with you and the Holy Spirit,
one God for ever and ever. Amen.

Some places to visit

Samlesbury Hall – the ancient home of the Southworth family and a Catholic safe house during penal times. Today it is open regularly, with a restaurant, garden and special exhibitions.
www.samlesburyhall.co.uk

St Mary and St John Southworth church, Preston New Road, Samlesbury – built in 1818, this small church contains a shrine to the martyr.

Douai – a relic of St John Southworth is kept in the shrine to the English Martyrs at the back of the Collegiate Church of St Peter. The location of the English College and of the saint's original burial is in the area around the Place Carnot.
www.ville-douai.fr

Lancaster Castle – where Southworth was briefly confined from 1626.
www.lancastercastle.com

The Clink – one of the London prisons where the saint was imprisoned.
www.clink.co.uk

St Edmund's College, Ware – now an independent school but formerly the location of the diocesan seminary, one of the successors of Douai. Visitors can visit the Douai Museum and the beautiful Pugin church. St John Southworth's body rested here between 1927 and 1930.
www.stedmundscollege.org

Tyburn Convent – a contemplative community of Benedictine nuns who perpetually adore the Blessed Sacrament and keep a shrine of the Martyrs, near to the spot where many of them suffered. Southworth's body was briefly brought here in 1930 en route to Westminster Cathedral.
www.tyburnconvent.org.uk

Westminster Cathedral – the final resting place of St John Southworth. There is a special celebration on his Feast (27 June), when the casket containing his body is taken into the centre of the nave. The area around the Cathedral is where Southworth ministered for many years, including during the plague of 1636.
www.westminstercathedral.org.uk

Select Bibliography

Godfrey Anstruther, O.P., *St John Southworth* (CTS, 1981).

Michael Archer, *St John Southworth* (CTS, 2010).

Stephen Porter, *The Plagues of London* (The History Press, 2008).

Albert B. Purdie, *Blessed John Southworth* (Burns & Oates, 1930).

E.E. Reynolds, *John Southworth – Priest and Martyr* (Burns & Oates, 1962).

'St John Southworth' by John Morrill, *Oxford Dictionary of National Biography* (2004).

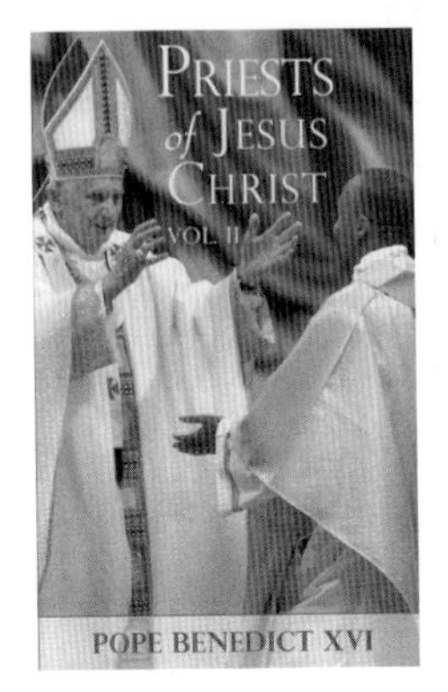

PRIESTS OF JESUS CHRIST V.II
Pope Benedict XVI
Gerard Skinner

A collection of texts taken from the various writings, speeches, prayers and homilies that Pope Benedict gave during the 'Year for Priests' 2008-9. These texts will, no doubt, inspire priests, seminarians, those discerning God's calling and others who appreciate the gift of priesthood in the mystery of Jesus Christ and give thanks to God for the same.

978-085439-806-5 £14.95

MINISTERS OF OUR JOY
Scriptural Meditations on Priestly Spirituality
Joseph Cardinal Ratzinger

Cardinal Ratzinger, as he was at the time of writing the reflections in this book, seeks to encourage and strengthen the desire and determination of priests to follow the Master more closely in accomplishing the Father's will, as well as in ministering the Good News to the brethren.

978-085439-783-9 £5.99

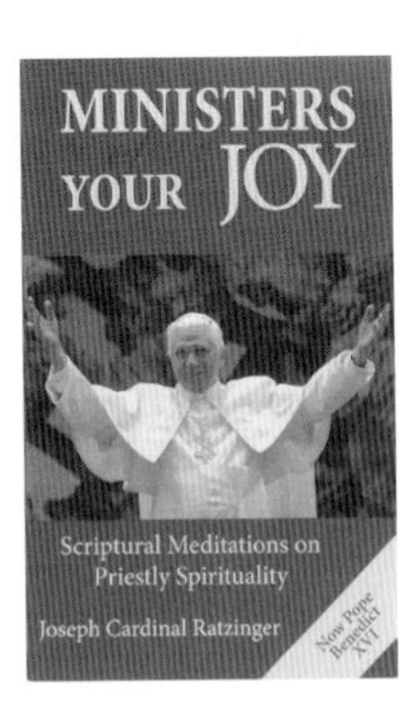

PRIESTHOOD
A Life Open to Christ
Compiled by Daniel P. Cronin

This book offers insights, for both ordained and lay people, into priestly life and ministry as experienced by 78 priests from around the world – from the Holy Father to one of the newest assistant priests and from the youngest to the oldest. Here are men who, writing from the depths of their hearts and in their own style, express what it means to be a priest.

978-085439-762-4 £10.00

VADEMECUM
Meditations on the Priesthood
Compiled by Stephen Moseling

A collection of quotations on the priesthood taken from scripture, the Fathers of the Church, Conciliar and Papal teaching and writers to the present day, to help priests and the laity reflect on the different aspects of the ordained priesthood.

978-085439-766-2 £15.95

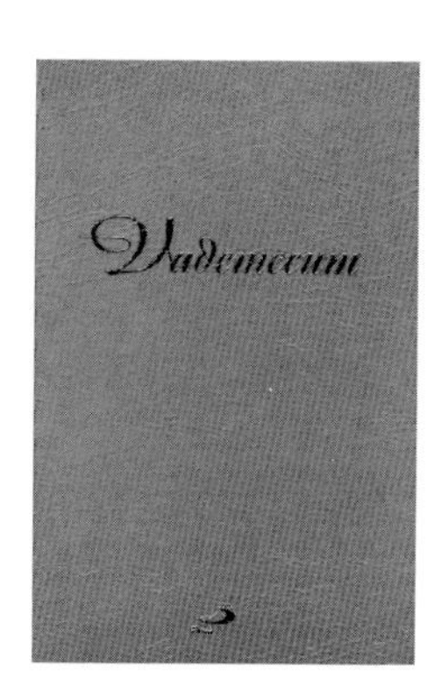

CATECHISM
with thoughts from the
Curé of Ars
Hugues d'Orfeuille,
trans. Alan Bancroft

Anxious to pass on "the elements of a serious theology" to young people and others, Hugues d'Orfeuille produced his own modern catechism, published in Paris in 1983. This is the first English translation.

978-085439-805-8 £9.95

ST JOHN MARY VIANNEY
THE CURÉ OF ARS
A Parish Priest for all the World
Joanna Bogle

St John Vianney grew up in a France devastated by the tragic events of the Revolution, and went on to become perhaps the most remarkable parish priest the Church has ever known. This book tells the story of his life – and how what was once a bleak rural parish become a centre of international pilgrimage.

978-085439-765-5 £5.25

THE REALM
An Unfashionable Essay on the Conversion of England
Aidan Nichols

Aidan Nichols tackles the current issues of church and state, religion and society, and what mission might mean today. He calls for a recovery of a distinct Christian identity and a confident faith which seeks to provide a common purpose for the realm.

978-085439-800-3 £9.95

CATHOLICISM IN UXBRIDGE
A Brief History
Nicholas Schofield

This brief history, written by the current parish priest, has been published to mark the 80th anniversary of the opening of the present church building. It is a fitting tribute to all who have worked, and those who continue to work, to build up the Kingdom of God in Uxbridge.

978-085439-825-6 £6.95

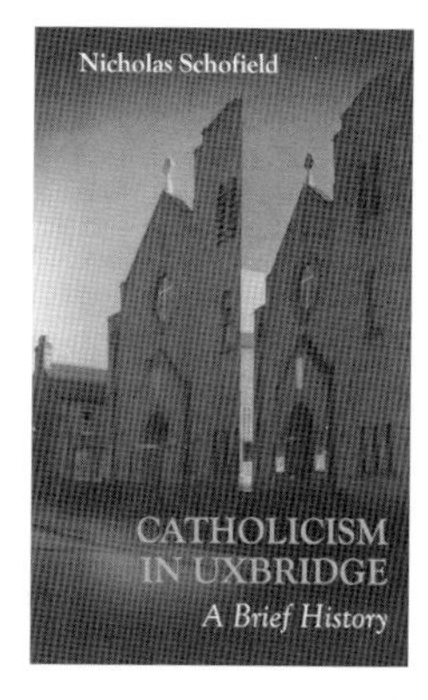

ST MARGARET CLITHEROW

Philip Caraman

This booklet offers an introduction to Margaret Clitherow, the remarkable Saint of York, and contains photographs of places from within the City of York associated with her.

978-085439-790-7 £1.50

THE ENGLISH VICARS APOSTOLIC 1688–1850

Nicholas Schofield, Gerard Skinner

Covering each district of the country and each Vicar Apostolic, the book provides an intimate portrait of the towering figures of bishops like Richard Challoner, John Milner, Thomas Walsh and many others.

978-190738-001-3 £14.95